Don't Be Afraid to Say Yes to God!

Pope Francis Speaks to Young People

With Reflections
by
Fr. Mike Schmitz

theWORD
among us®
press

Published by The Word Among Us Press
7115 Guilford Road
Frederick, Maryland 21704
www.wau.org

22 21 20 19 18   1 2 3 4 5

ISBN: 978-1-59325-328-8
eISBN: 978-1-59325-503-9

Pope Francis's homilies and addresses are taken from
the Vatican translation and can be found on the Vatican website,
www.vatican.va. Used with permission of
Libreria Editrice Vaticana.

Scripture texts used in this work are taken from The Catholic Edition
of the Revised Standard Version Bible, copyright © 1965, 1966 by
the Division of Christian Education of the National Council of the
Churches of Christ in the United States of America.
Used with permission. All rights reserved.

Cover design by Faceout Studios
Cover photo: Massimo Valicchia/Alamy Stock Photo

Made and printed in the United States of America
Library of Congress Control Number: 2017964107

Contents

Letter to Young People

Letter to Young People on the Occasion of the Presentation of the Preparatory Document of the Fifteenth Ordinary General Assembly of the Synod of Bishops, Given at the Vatican, January 13, 2017

My Dear Young People,

I am pleased to announce that in October 2018 a Synod of Bishops will take place to treat the topic: "Young People, the Faith and Vocational Discernment." I wanted you to be the center of attention, because you are in my heart. Today, the Preparatory Document is being presented, a document which I am also entrusting to you as your "compass" on this synodal journey.

I am reminded of the words which God spoke to Abraham: "Go from your country and your kindred and your father's house to the land that I will show you." (Genesis 12:1). These words are now also addressed to you. They are words of a Father who invites you to "go," to set out towards a future which is unknown but one which will surely lead to fulfillment, a future towards which He Himself accompanies you. I invite you to hear God's voice resounding in your heart through the breath of the Holy Spirit.

When God said to Abram, "Go!" what did he want to say? He certainly did not say to distance himself from his family or withdraw from the world. Abram received a compelling invitation, a challenge, to leave everything and go to a new land. What is this "new land" for us today, if not a more just and friendly society which you, young people, deeply desire and wish to build to the very ends of the earth?

But unfortunately, today, "Go!" also has a different meaning, namely, that of abuse of power, injustice and war. Many among you are subjected to the real threat of violence and forced to flee your native land. Their cry goes up to God, like that of Israel, when the people were enslaved and oppressed by Pharaoh (cf. Exodus 2:23).

I would also remind you of the words that Jesus once said to the disciples who asked him: "Teacher [. . .], where are you staying?" He replied, "Come and see" (John 1:38). Jesus looks at you and invites you to go with him. Dear young people, have you noticed this look towards you? Have you heard this voice? Have you felt this urge to undertake this journey? I am sure that, despite the noise and confusion seemingly prevalent in the world, this call continues to resonate in the depths of your heart so as to open it to joy in its fullness. This will be possible to the extent that, even with professional guides, you will learn how to undertake a journey of discernment to discover God's plan in your life. Even when the journey is uncertain and you fall, God, rich in mercy, will extend his hand to pick you up.

In Kraków, at the opening of the last World Youth Day, I asked you several times: "Can we change things?" And you shouted: "Yes!" That shout came from your young and youthful hearts, which do not tolerate injustice and cannot bow to a "throw-away culture" nor give in to the globalization of indifference. Listen to the cry arising from your inner selves! Even when you feel, like the prophet Jeremiah, the inexperience of youth, God encourages you to go where He sends you: "Do not be afraid, [. . .], because I am with you to deliver you" (Jeremiah 1:8).

A better world can be built also as a result of your efforts, your desire to change and your generosity. Do not be afraid to listen to the Spirit who proposes bold choices; do not delay when your conscience asks you to take risks in following the Master. The Church also wishes to listen to your voice, your sensitivities and your faith; even your doubts and your criticism. Make your voice heard, let it resonate in communities and let it be heard by your shepherds of souls. St. Benedict urged the abbots to consult, even the young, before any important decision, because "the Lord often reveals to the younger what is best" (*Rule of St. Benedict*, III, 3). Such is the case, even in the journey of this Synod. My brother bishops and I want even more to "work with you for your joy" (2 Corinthians 1:24). I entrust you to Mary of Nazareth, a young person like yourselves, whom God beheld lovingly, so she might take your hand and guide you to the joy of fully and generously responding to God's call with the words: "Here I am" (cf. Luke 1:38).

With paternal affection,

FRANCIS

Prayer for Young People in View of the Forthcoming Synod of Bishops 2018

Lord Jesus, in journeying towards the Synod, your Church turns her attention to all the young people of the world. We pray that they might boldly take charge of their lives, aim for the most beautiful and profound things of life, and always keep their hearts unencumbered. Accompanied by wise and generous guides, help them respond to the call you make to each of them, to realize a proper plan of life and achieve happiness.

Keep their hearts open to dreaming great dreams and make them concerned for the good of others. Like the Beloved Disciple, may they stand at the foot of the cross, to receive your Mother as a gift from you. May they be witnesses to your resurrection and be aware that you are at their side as they joyously proclaim you as Lord. Amen.

—*L'Osservatore Romano*, April 14, 2017

Introduction

July 2017 marked the two-hundredth anniversary of the birth of Henry David Thoreau. He lived only forty-five short years on this planet and rarely ventured far from Concord, the small town in Massachusetts where he was born. And yet, while he never wrote any symphonies, never built anything marking the New York City skyline, never invented anything or ran an important company, this man influenced not only his own generation of artists and builders, politicians and business people, he has also influenced many who have lived in the two centuries since his birth. What was it about this man and his thinking that has had such an impact on so many? A quote from his book *Walden* demonstrates Thoreau's ability to connect with his contemporaries and with us: "The mass of men live lives of quiet desperation." Think about that for a moment. Does this sound like people you know? Does this sound like you? Henry David Thoreau placed his finger on one of the hidden and unspoken truths that many of us experience on a daily basis.

Of course, these days we are super good at avoiding deep thoughts about desperation, or meaning, or similar unsettling ideas. We can distract ourselves with our personalized and immediate music stations (think Pandora or Spotify), our personalized and immediate TV shows or movies (think Netflix or Hulu), or our personalized and immediate websites (think Facebook, Twitter, or Instagram). None of those things are bad. Access to great music, entertainment, and digital connection with our friends and family is a gift! But too often these things not only distract us from having to think about the kind of life we are living, but they also *contribute* to our "quiet desperation."

Think about it. How many of us have missed enjoying a gorgeous summer afternoon outside because it was easier to get sucked into the latest YouTube rabbit trail? How many of us showed up late for a meeting with friends (or skipped it altogether) because we got sucked into the latest series on Netflix? How many of us were exhausted and wanted to go to sleep, but got into bed and then spent the next forty-five minutes scrolling through other people's SnapStories?

Inventing the Meaning of Life

Thoreau noted this tendency to distract ourselves from living life and our tendency to avoid noticing our distraction. These tendencies are even more pronounced now than they were in Henry's day. We see this not only in our quest for distraction, but also in our search—or, more accurately, failure to search—for meaning.

One of the great tragedies of our time is a reluctance to even care about ultimate meaning. I mean, think about this term: "ultimate meaning." Doesn't it sound old-fashioned? Doesn't it sound naïve? Doesn't it sound like the kind of thing that philosophers and priests would talk about, but no one could actually discover and live? The "meaning of life" is something that a person has to invent for themselves, right? It certainly seems so.

Back in 1992, United States Supreme Court Justice Anthony Kennedy wrote that at the heart of liberty is "the right to define one's own concept of existence, of meaning, of the universe, and of the mystery of human life." He seems to be saying that a person does not *discover* the meaning of life, but that we have to invent it for ourselves. That seems like a tall order for anyone, much less for those of us who live in the real world.

But it is not merely the fact that inventing the meaning of life would be difficult. We all recognize that we have come into a world that already exists. We have been born into a world that already has meaning. We are not here by accident. We are not the masters of our own destiny in every way imaginable. We are inheritors of a world that exists outside of us and would continue to exist without us. We are here to discover the meaning of a life we did not create and to live that life . . . not of quiet desperation, but of profound peace and joy.

But who can offer us direction to discover this kind of life? Thoreau diagnosed the problem, but who has the cure? Um, well . . . the world would have us believe that everyone does. It seems as if there isn't a person alive who doesn't have their own version of the meaning of life.

Some people claim that we live in an age of hyper information. I guess I wouldn't argue with that; we have more information at our fingertips than many of us know what to do with. But I think that the bigger issue is that we live in an age of hyper *opinion*. We don't merely have people willing to share the data with us, but pretty much everybody is willing to tell us what it means.

Relationships vs. Truth

I think that this is why relationships are so over-valued and so under-lived in our day. While we all like the personalized and immediate media and lifestyle, they lead to a life disconnected from other people. In our great loneliness, we might pause and look up from our devices only to find that everyone else is buried in theirs. Simply to *connect* with someone—anyone, in this sea of anonymity—is enough to make a person abandon what they know is true and cling to the other.

Here's what I mean—and I've seen this over and over in my work with teens and college students. Let's say that there is a guy who has faith in Jesus Christ and has a relatively good understanding that there are certain things that are right and certain things that are wrong. But then he becomes friends with a person who sometimes does those things that are wrong and he thinks, "My friend is a good person. He isn't evil. In fact, he's a lot nicer in other areas than many Christians I know!"

Do you see what has happened? Rather than make the critical distinction between the sinner and the sin, the relationship takes precedence over what the person knows to be true. How many of us are willing to change what we believe about the meaning of life (and what constitutes a well-lived life) simply because of a relationship? I think that this comes from the fact that in a world filled with contrasting and contradictory voices, we trust those people we know.

This is why a book like this is so important.

Pope Francis has shown us that he can be trusted. He is a person of *relationships*. He is a person of encounter and accompaniment. What is more, he is also the shepherd given to us by the Holy Spirit in order to teach and guide us. When Pope Francis teaches us, we have the twofold sense that (1) he knows the Lord and he knows people, and (2) we can trust him.

This trusted teacher and follower of Jesus Christ keeps reminding us that our lives are not meaningless!

He continues to call all of us to "put on Christ" in a new and definitive way. Not, as so many of us do, the way one wears a team jersey, putting it on for game day but then wearing regular clothes for the rest of the week. Pope Francis reminds us that we are called to live in Christ and his Holy Spirit, day in and day out, regardless of any hyper opinions we may encounter, or relationships we may form. He reminds us that we are called to consistently and faithfully live and speak in such a way as to be found in Christ.

This is the "secret" that Pope Francis brings to our attention throughout this book. We are not alone. Jesus Christ is the true

God who loves us perfectly and infinitely and *right now*. God is not waiting for us to be better to start loving us. God loves us— he loves *you*—right now.

This is the love that Jesus reveals. This is the love that Pope Francis wants us to know. It is the only thing that can, in the final analysis, save us from a life of quiet desperation. This is the love (and truth) that can enable us to live in the freedom and joy of the sons and daughters of God.

In Christ,

Father Mike

Chapter 1

COME, FOLLOW ME

The Lord of Risk

My friends, Jesus is the Lord of risk; he is the Lord of the eternal "more." Jesus is not the Lord of comfort, security, and ease. Following Jesus demands a good dose of courage, a readiness to trade in the sofa for a pair of walking shoes and to set out on new and uncharted paths. To blaze trails that open up new horizons capable of spreading joy. . . .

To take the path of the "craziness" of our God, who teaches us to encounter him in the hungry, the thirsty, the naked, the sick, the friend in trouble, the prisoner, the refugee and the migrant, and our neighbors who feel abandoned.

To take the path of our God, who encourages us to be politicians, thinkers, social activists. The God who encourages us to devise an economy marked by greater solidarity than our own.

In all the settings in which you find yourselves, God's love invites you bring the Good News, making of your own lives a gift to him and to others. This means being courageous, this means being free!

—Prayer Vigil with Young People, World Youth Day,
Kraków, Poland, July 30, 2016

—For Reflection—

What does it mean for you, personally, to take a risk for God?

What is he asking of you? Is there anything holding you back?

How can you trade in the comfort of the couch for the courage needed to chart new paths?

Victory in the Cross

What has the cross given to those who have gazed upon it and to those who have touched it? What has the cross left in each one of us? You see, it gives us a treasure that no one else can give: the certainty of the faithful love which God has for us. A love so great that it enters into our sin and forgives it, enters into our suffering and gives us the strength to bear it. It is a love which enters into death to conquer it and to save us.

The cross of Christ contains all the love of God; there we find his immeasurable mercy. This is a love in which we can place all our trust, in which we can believe.

Dear young people, let us entrust ourselves to Jesus, let us give ourselves over to him (cf. *Lumen Fideli,* 16), because he never disappoints anyone! Only in Christ crucified and risen can we find salvation and redemption. With him, evil, suffering, and death do not have the last word, because he gives us hope and life: he has transformed the cross from being an instrument of hate, defeat, and death to being a sign of love, victory, triumph, and life.

—Way of the Cross with Young People, World Youth Day,
Rio de Janeiro, Brazil, July 26, 2013

—For Reflection—

Are you convicted of Christ's love and mercy, demonstrated by his dying on the cross for you?

Do you believe in his victory over sin—over your sin in particular?

Does this conviction lead you to surrender everything to him?

Called by Name

Let us listen to the words that Jesus spoke to Zacchaeus, which seem to be meant for us today, for each one of us: "Come down, for I must stay at your house today" (Luke 19:5). "Come down, for I must stay with you today. Open to me the door of your heart." Jesus extends the same invitation to you: "I must stay at your house today." . . .

[Jesus] wants to enter your homes, to dwell in your daily lives: in your studies, your first years of work, your friendships and affections, your hopes and dreams. How greatly he desires that you bring all this to him in prayer! How much he hopes that, in all the "contacts" and "chats" of each day, pride of place be given to the golden thread of prayer! How much he wants his word to be able to speak to you day after day, so that you can make his Gospel your own, so that it can serve as a compass for you on the highways of life!

In asking to come to your house, Jesus *calls you*, as he did Zacchaeus, *by name*. All of us, Jesus calls by name. Your name is precious to him. . . . Let us listen once more to the voice of Jesus as he calls us by name.

—Homily at Mass, World Youth Day,
Kraków, Poland, July 31, 2016

—For Reflection—

Does your love for God and others flow first from his love for you?

Do you want him to call you by name—or do you resist him?

How can you learn to recognize his voice as he speaks to you and calls you to follow him?

Surprised by God

True love is both loving and letting oneself be loved. It is harder to let ourselves be loved than it is to love. That is why it is so hard to achieve the perfect love of God, because we can love him but the important thing is to let ourselves be loved by him.

True love is being open to that love which was there first and catches us by surprise. If all you have is information, you are closed to surprises. Love makes you open to surprises. Love is always a surprise, because it starts with a dialogue between two persons: the one who loves and the one who is loved.

We say that God is the God of surprises, because he always loved us first and he waits to take us by surprise. God surprises us. Let's allow ourselves to be surprised by God. Let's not have the psychology of a computer, thinking that we know everything. What do I mean? Think for a moment: the computer has all the answers: never a surprise. In the challenge of love, God shows up with surprises.

Think of St. Matthew (cf. Matthew 9:9-13). He was a good businessman. He also betrayed his country because he collected taxes from the Jews and paid them to the Romans. He was loaded with money and he collected taxes. Then Jesus comes along, looks at him and says: "Come, follow me." Matthew couldn't believe it. . . .

That morning, when Matthew was going off to work and said goodbye to his wife, he never thought that he was going to return in a hurry, without money, to tell his wife to prepare a banquet. The banquet for the one who loved him first, who surprised him with something important, more important than all the money he had.

So let yourselves be surprised by God! Don't be afraid of surprises, afraid that they will shake you up. They make us insecure, but they change the direction we are going in. True love makes you "burn life," even at the risk of coming up empty-handed. Think of Saint Francis: he left everything, he died with empty hands, but with a full heart.

—Meeting with Young People, Manila, Philippines, January 18, 2015

—For Reflection—

Do you let yourself be surprised by God or do you want everything plotted out so that nothing interferes with your plans?

What would it take for you to let go and let God show you the next step in **his** plan for you? Is fear holding you back?

Can you name that fear and offer it to God?

Pressing Forward

The meeting of the two women [Mary and Elizabeth], one young and the other elderly, is filled with the presence of the Holy Spirit and charged with joy and wonder (cf. Luke 1:40-45). The two mothers, like the children they bear, practically dance for joy. Elizabeth, impressed by Mary's faith, cries out: "Blessed is she who believed that there would be a fulfillment of what was spoken to her by the Lord" (verse 45).

One of the great gifts that the Virgin received was certainly that of faith. Belief in God is a priceless gift, but one that has to be received. Elizabeth blesses Mary for this, and she in turn responds with the song of the Magnificat (cf. Luke 1:46-55), in which we find the words: "The Mighty One has done great things for me" (verse 49).

Mary's is a revolutionary prayer, the song of a faith-filled young woman conscious of her limits, yet confident in God's mercy. . . .

When God touches the heart of a young man or woman, they become capable of doing tremendous things. The "great things" that the Almighty accomplished in the life of Mary speak also to our own journey in life, which is not a meaningless meandering, but a pilgrimage that, for all its uncertainties and sufferings, can find its fulfillment in God (cf. Angelus Address, August 15, 2015).

You may say to me: "But Father, I have my limits, I am a sinner, what can I do?" When the Lord calls us, he doesn't stop at what we are or what we have done. On the contrary, at the very moment that he calls us, he is looking ahead to everything we can do, all the love we are capable of giving.

Like the young Mary, you can allow your life to become a means for making the world a better place. Jesus is calling you to leave your mark in life, your mark on history, both your own and that of so many others (cf. Address at the Vigil, Kraków, July 30, 2016).

—Message for the Thirty-Second World Youth Day, February 27, 2017

—For Reflection—

What are some of the great things that the Mighty One has done for you?

Do you truly believe, as Mary did, that the Lord will fulfill what he has promised you in your own prayer and in Scripture?

Do you trust and believe that the Lord will work through you, beyond your own capabilities and in spite of your sinfulness?

Following Jesus' Path

The Gospel does not only concern religion. . . . It concerns the world, society, and human civilization. The Gospel is God's message of salvation for mankind. When we say "message of salvation," this is not simply a way of speaking, these are not mere words or empty words like so many today. Mankind truly needs to be saved!

We see it everyday when we flip through newspapers or watch the news on television; but we also see it around us, in people, in situations; and we see it in ourselves! Each one of us needs to be saved! We cannot do it alone! We need to be saved! Saved from what? From evil. Evil is at work, it does its job. However, evil is not invincible and a Christian does not give up when confronted by evil. . . .

Our secret is that God is greater than evil: this is true! God is greater than evil. God is infinite love, boundless mercy, and that Love has conquered evil at its root through the death and resurrection of Christ. This is the Gospel, the Good News: God's love has won! Christ died on the cross for our sins and rose again. With him we can fight evil and conquer every day.

Do we believe this or not? . . . If I believe that Jesus has conquered evil and saved me, I must follow along the path of Jesus for my whole life.

—Meeting with the Young People of Umbria, Assisi, Italy, October 4, 2013

—For Reflection—

Are you convinced of humanity's need for God's mercy and love?

In what areas of your life do you need to allow God to save you?

Will you let God lead you down his path for your life?

God Cheers Us On

We are God's beloved children, always. So you can see that not to accept ourselves, to live glumly, to be negative, means not to recognize our deepest identity. It is like walking away when God wants to look at me, trying to reveal his dream to me. God loves us the way we are, and no sin, fault, or mistake of ours makes him change his mind.

As far as Jesus is concerned—as the Gospel shows—no one is unworthy of, or far from, his thoughts. No one is insignificant. He loves all of us with a special love; for him all of us are important: *you* are important! God counts on you for what you are, not for what you possess. In his eyes the clothes you wear or the kind of cell phone you use are of absolutely no concern. He doesn't care whether you are stylish or not; he cares about you, just as you are! In his eyes, you are precious, and your value is inestimable.

At times in our lives, we aim lower rather than higher. At those times, it is good to realize that God remains faithful, even obstinate, in his love for us. The fact is, he loves us even more than we love ourselves. He believes in us even more than we believe in ourselves. He is always "cheering us on"; he is our biggest fan.

He is there for us, waiting with patience and hope, even when we turn in on ourselves and brood over our troubles and past injuries. But such brooding is unworthy of our spiritual stature! It is a kind of *virus* infecting and blocking everything; it closes doors and prevents us from getting up and starting over.

God, on the other hand, is hopelessly hopeful! He believes that we can always get up, and he hates to see us glum and gloomy. It is sad to see young people who are glum. Because we are always his beloved sons and daughters.

Let us be mindful of this at the dawn of each new day. It will do us good to pray every morning: "Lord, I thank you for loving me; I am sure that you love me; help me to be in love with my own life! Not with my faults that need to be corrected, but with life itself, which is a great gift, for it is a time to love and to be loved."

—Homily at Mass, World Youth Day, Kraków, Poland, July 31, 2016

—For Reflection—

Is your identity rooted in God's love for you?

Do you truly believe that you are God's beloved child? When you think of him gazing at you, how do you picture him?

Do you let God love you in your brokenness?

Overcoming the Paralysis of Shame

We can imagine what was going on in [Zacchaeus'] heart before he climbed that sycamore [see Luke 19:1-10]. It must have been quite a struggle—on one hand, a healthy curiosity and desire to know Jesus; on the other, the risk of appearing completely ridiculous. Zacchaeus was a public figure, a man of power, but deeply hated. He knew that, in trying to climb that tree, he would become a laughingstock to all. Yet he mastered his shame, because the attraction of Jesus was more powerful. You know what happens when someone is so attractive that we fall in love with them: we end up ready to do things we would never have even thought of doing. Something similar took place in the heart of Zacchaeus, when he realized that Jesus was so important that he would do anything for him, since Jesus alone could pull him out of the mire of sin and discontent.

The paralysis of shame did not have the upper hand. The Gospel tells us that Zacchaeus "ran ahead," "climbed" the tree, and then, when Jesus called him, he "hurried down" (Luke 19:4, 6). He took a risk; he put his life on the line.

For us, too, this is the secret of joy: not to stifle a healthy curiosity, but to take a risk, because life is not meant to be tucked away. When it comes to Jesus, we cannot sit around waiting with arms folded; he offers us life—we can't respond by thinking about it or "texting" a few words!

—Homily at Mass, World Youth Day, Kraków, Poland, July 31, 2016

—For Reflection—

If you want to get closer to Jesus, you run the risk of appearing different from others. Are you willing to take that risk? Or are you more attracted to your own comforts and thoughts than you are to Jesus?

What can you learn from Zacchaeus about taking action for Jesus in your own life?

False Illusions Versus Fullness of Life

I am saddened to see young people who walk around glumly as if life had no meaning. . . . . It is also hard, and troubling, to see young people who waste their lives looking for thrills or a feeling of being alive by taking dark paths and in the end having to pay for it—and pay dearly.

Think of so many young people you know, who have chosen this path. It is disturbing to see young people squandering some of the best years of their lives, wasting their energies running after peddlers of false illusions, and they do exist, (where I come from, we call them "vendors of smoke"), who rob you of what is best in you. This pains me. . . .

To find fulfillment, to gain new life, there is a way, a way that is not for sale, that cannot be purchased, a way that is not a thing or an object, but a person. His name is Jesus Christ . . . .

Jesus can give you true passion for life. Jesus can inspire us not to settle for less, but to give the very best of ourselves. Jesus challenges us, spurs us on, and helps us keep trying whenever we are tempted to give up. Jesus pushes us to keep our sights high and to dream of great things.

You might say to me, "But Father, it is so difficult to dream of great things, it is so difficult to rise up, to be always moving forwards and upwards. Father, I am weak, I fall, and I try but so many times I fall down." Mountaineers, as they climb mountains, sing a very beautiful song whose words go like this: "In the art of climbing, it is not important that you do not fall down, but that you do not stay down."

If you are weak, if you fall, look up a little for there is Jesus' hand extended to you as he says: "Rise up, come with me." "And what if I fall again?" Rise again. "And what if I fall yet again?" Rise yet again. Peter once asked the Lord: "Lord, how many times?" And the reply came: "seventy times seven." The hand of Jesus is always extended, ready to lift us up again when we fall.

—Welcoming Ceremony, World Youth Day, Kraków, Poland, July 28, 2016

—For Reflection—

Has Jesus ever inspired you to live your life passionately for him? If not, have you asked him to inspire you?

Whether you feel inspired each moment of your day or not, what keeps you from responding to Jesus when he says, "Rise up, come with me"?

No Couch Potato

According to Luke's Gospel, once Mary has received the message of the angel and said "yes" to the call to become the Mother of the Savior, she sets out in haste to visit her cousin Elizabeth, who was in the sixth month of her pregnancy (cf. 1:36, 39). Mary is very young; what she was told is a great gift, but it also entails great challenges.

The Lord assured her of his presence and support, yet many things remain obscure in her mind and heart. Yet Mary does not shut herself up at home or let herself be paralyzed by fear or pride. Mary is not the type that, to be comfortable, needs a good sofa where she can feel safe and sound. She is no couch potato! (cf. Address at the Vigil, Kraków , July 30, 2016). If her elderly cousin needs a hand, she does not hesitate, but immediately sets off.

It was a long way to the house of Elizabeth, about 150 kilometers [about 93 miles]. But the young woman from Nazareth, led by the Holy Spirit, knows no obstacles. Surely, those days of journeying helped her to meditate on the marvelous event of which she was a part.

So it is with us, whenever we set out on pilgrimage. Along the way, the events of our own lives come to mind, we learn to appreciate their meaning and we discern our vocation, which then becomes clear in the encounter with God and in service to others.

—Message for the Thirty-Second World Youth Day, February 27, 2017

—For Reflection—

As you journey through life, do you take time to reflect on what God has given you and where he is calling you?

Where is the Holy Spirit leading you in your life right now?

Do you go with haste to serve others as Mary did?

Chapter 2

●

COURAGE

No Barriers

How hard it is to accept a "God who is rich in mercy" (Ephesians 2:4)! People will try to block you, to make you think that God is distant, rigid, and insensitive, good to the good and bad to the bad. Instead, our heavenly Father "makes his sun rise on the evil and on the good" (Matthew 5:45). He demands of us real courage: the courage to be *more powerful than evil* by loving everyone, even our enemies.

People may laugh at you because you believe in the gentle and unassuming power of mercy. But do not be afraid. . . .

People may judge you to be dreamers, because you believe in a new humanity, one that rejects hatred between peoples, one that refuses to see borders as barriers and can cherish its own traditions without being self-centered or small-minded. Don't be discouraged: with a smile and open arms, you proclaim hope and you are a blessing for our one human family. . . .

Jesus looks beyond the faults and sees the person. He does not halt before bygone evil, but sees future good. His gaze remains constant, even when it is not met; it seeks the way of unity and communion. In no case does it halt at appearances, but looks to the heart.

Jesus looks to our hearts, your heart, my heart. With this gaze of Jesus, you can help bring about another humanity, without looking for acknowledgment but seeking goodness for its own sake, content to maintain a pure heart and to fight peaceably for honesty and justice.

—Homily at Mass, World Youth Day, Kraków, Poland, July 31, 2016

—For Reflection—

Have you ever seen someone acting for the good of someone else, demonstrating "goodness for its own sake"? What impact did that have on you?

Are there role models in your life who do the same, not seeking to have their good deeds acknowledged, but acting, instead, from a pure heart? How can you imitate them as they imitate Christ?

The Courage to Be Happy

To be blessed means to be happy. Tell me: Do you really want to be happy? In an age when we are constantly being enticed by vain and empty illusions of happiness, we risk settling for less and "thinking small" when it comes to the meaning of life. Think big instead! . . .

If you are really open to the deepest aspirations of your hearts, you will realize that you possess an unquenchable thirst for happiness, and this will allow you to expose and reject the "low cost" offers and approaches all around you.

When we look only for success, pleasure and possessions, and we turn these into idols, we may well have moments of exhilaration, an illusory sense of satisfaction, but ultimately we become enslaved, never satisfied, always looking for more. It is a tragic thing to see a young person who "has everything" but is weary and weak.

St. John, writing to young people, told them: "You are strong, and the word of God abides in you, and you have overcome the evil one" (1 John 2:14). Young people who choose Christ *are* strong: they are fed by his word and they do not need to "stuff themselves" with other things!

Have the courage to swim against the tide. Have the courage to be truly happy! Say no to an ephemeral, superficial and throw-away culture, a culture that assumes that you are incapable of taking on responsibility and facing the great challenges of life!

—Message for the Twenty-Ninth World Youth Day, January 21, 2014

—For Reflection—

Do you sometimes look for happiness by seeking success or pleasure or possessions?

Do these things really fill the "unquenchable thirst for happiness" that exists in your soul?

What are a few ways you can choose Christ so as to be filled with him rather than the things that do not last?

Jesus and You, Carrying the Cross

According to an ancient Roman tradition, while fleeing the city during the persecutions of Nero, St. Peter saw Jesus who was travelling in the opposite direction, that is, toward the city, and asked him in amazement: "Lord, where are you going?" Jesus' response was: "I am going to Rome to be crucified again." At that moment, Peter understood that he had to follow the Lord with courage, to the very end.

But he also realized that he would never be alone on the journey. Jesus, who had loved him even unto death, would always be with him. Jesus, with his cross, walks with us and takes upon himself our fears, our problems, and our sufferings, even those which are deepest and most painful. . . .

On the cross, Jesus is united with those who are persecuted for their religion, for their beliefs, or simply for the color of their skin. On the cross, Jesus is united with so many young people who have lost faith in political institutions, because they see in them only selfishness and corruption. He unites himself with those young people who have lost faith in the Church, or even in God because of the counterwitness of Christians and ministers of the Gospel.

How our inconsistencies make Jesus suffer! The cross of Christ bears the suffering and the sin of mankind, including our own. Jesus accepts all this with open arms, bearing on his shoulders our crosses and saying to us: "Have courage! You do not carry your cross alone! I carry it with you. I have overcome death and I have come to give you hope, to give you life" (cf. John 3:16).

—Way of the Cross with Young People, World Youth Day, Rio de Janeiro, Brazil, July 26, 2013

—For Reflection—

Do you run away from certain areas of your life because you are afraid to face them? Do you let Jesus into those areas?

What sufferings are you holding onto, refusing to let Jesus help you carry them?

How might Jesus want to give you life through these crosses?

The Courage to Reach Out

When a religion becomes a "little world," it loses the best that it has, it stops worshiping God, believing in God. It becomes a little world of words, of prayers, of "I am good and you are bad," of moral rules and regulations. If I have my ideology, my way of thinking, and you have yours, I lock myself up in this little world of ideology.

Open hearts and open minds. If you are different than I am, then why don't we talk? Why do we always throw stones at one another over what separates us, what makes us different? Why don't we extend a hand where we have common ground? Why not try to speak about what we have in common, and then we can talk about where we differ. . . .

In Buenos Aires, in a new parish in an extremely poor area, a group of university students were building some rooms for the parish. So the parish priest said to me: "Why don't you come one Saturday and I'll introduce them to you?" They were building on Saturdays and Sundays. They were young men and women from the university. So I arrived, I saw them, and they were introduced to me: "This is the architect. He's Jewish. This one is Communist. This one is a practicing Catholic." They were all different, yet they were all working for the common good.

This is called social friendship, where everyone works for the common good. . . . And this is what I'm asking you today: to find ways of building social friendship.

—Address to Students, Havana, Cuba, September 20, 2015

—For Reflection—

Consider the people in your life who do not believe what you believe, or who have a different world view than you. Do you feel the Lord is inviting you to grow in friendship with them?

What are some good ways to find common ground in those relationships?

Bet on the Future with Jesus

Dear young people, the heart of the human being aspires to great things, lofty values, deep friendships, ties that are strengthened rather than broken by the trials of life. The human being aspires to love and to be loved. This is our deepest aspiration: to love and be loved; and definitively.

The culture of the temporary does not honor our freedom, but deprives us of our true destiny, of our truest and most authentic goals. It is a piecemeal life. It is sad to reach a certain age, to look back over the journey we have made and find that it was made up of different pieces, without unity, without decisiveness: everything temporary. . . .

Do not allow yourselves to be robbed of the will to build great and lasting things in your life! This is what leads you forward. Do not content yourselves with little goals. Aspire to happiness, have courage, the courage to go outside of yourselves and bet on the fullness of your future together with Jesus.

—Meeting with the Young People of the Italian Dioceses
of Abruzzi and Molise, July 5, 2014

—For Reflection—

What hopes do you have for your future?

What do you think will bring you the fullness of life in your future with Jesus? (Do not be afraid to dream big!)

How is the Lord inviting you to love and to be loved so that you can you form friendships that will endure through the trials of life?

Don't Be Discouraged

[God] helps us not to become discouraged in the face of difficulties, not to consider them insurmountable; and then, trusting in Him, you will again cast the nets for a surprising and abundant catch, you will have courage and hope. . . .

Courage and hope are qualities that everyone has, but they are most befitting in young people: courage and hope. The future is surely in the hands of God, the hands of a provident Father. This does not mean denying difficulties and problems, but seeing them, yes, as temporary and surmountable. Difficulties, crises, can, with God's help and the goodwill of all, be overcome, defeated, transformed.

—Meeting with the Young People of the Italian Dioceses
of Abruzzi and Molise, July 5, 2014

—For Reflection—

What are some difficulties in your life that seem insurmountable right now?

How is the Lord inviting you to have hope and courage in the midst of these difficulties?

Can you consider some ways that good could come out of these struggles?

Not Alone

Some people might think: "I have no particular preparation, how can I go and proclaim the Gospel?" My dear friend, your fear is not so very different from that of Jeremiah, . . . when he was called by God to be a prophet. "Ah, Lord God! Behold, I do not know how to speak, for I am only a youth." God says the same thing to you as he said to Jeremiah: "Be not afraid . . . for I am with you to deliver you" (1:7, 8). He is with us!

"Do not be afraid!" When we go to proclaim Christ, it is he himself who goes before us and guides us. When he sent his disciples on mission, he promised: "I am with you always" (Matthew 28:20). And this is also true for us! Jesus never leaves anyone alone! He always accompanies us.

—Homily, World Youth Day,
Rio de Janeiro, Brazil, July 28, 2013

———For Reflection———

Pope Francis tells us to not be afraid because it is Christ who goes before us and guides us. Knowing this, why is it important to open your heart to Jesus *before* going out and proclaiming the Gospel?

In what ways can you more fully open your heart to receive the love of Christ?

How has Christ already shown you that he is accompanying you on your journey?

Backbone

I would like to reflect on two fundamental values: freedom and service. First of all: be free people! What do I mean? Perhaps it is thought that freedom means doing everything one likes, or seeing how far one can go by trying drunkenness and overcoming boredom. This is not freedom.

Freedom means being able to think about what we do, being able to assess what is good and what is bad, these are the types of conduct that lead to development; it means always opting for the good. Let us be free for goodness. And in this do not be afraid to go against the tide, even if it is not easy! Always being free to choose goodness is demanding but it will make you into people with a backbone who can face life, people with courage and patience (*parrhesia* and *ypomoné*).

The second word is service. In your schools you take part in various activities that accustom you to not retreating into yourselves or into your own small world, but rather to being open to others, especially the poorest and neediest. They accustom you to working hard to improve the world in which we live. Be men and women with others and for others: true champions at the service of others.

—Address to the Students of the Jesuit Schools of Italy and Albania,
Paul VI Audience Hall, June 7, 2013

—For Reflection—

Pope St. John Paul II said, "Freedom consists not in doing what we like, but in having the right to do what we ought." In what ways is the Lord inviting you to experience true freedom by saying no to what you want in order to say yes to what is right?

How is the Lord inviting you to serve others and step outside of yourself?

Chapter 3

•

FORGIVENESS

Come to the Party

The prodigal son, the son who left home, spent all his money—everything he had—betrayed his father and his family, betrayed everything. At a certain moment, out of necessity, but full of shame, he decided to return. He thought about how he would ask for his father's forgiveness. He thought he would say: "Father, I have sinned, I have done all these wrong things, so I want to be your servant, not your son," and lots of other fine things.

But the Gospel tells us that the father saw his son coming from afar. Why did he see him? Because every day he used to go out onto the terrace to see if his son would return. The father embraced him: he did not let his son speak; he did not let him say all that he had rehearsed, and he did not allow him to even ask for forgiveness. Then he went off to organize a party.

This is the party that God enjoys: whenever we return home, whenever we return to him. "But Father, I am a sinful man, a sinful woman . . . " All the better, he is waiting for you! All the better, and he will throw a party! Jesus himself tells us that there will be more celebration in heaven over one sinner who turns back than for a hundred of the righteous who remain at home.

None of us knows what life will bring us. And you, dear young friends, are asking: "What is in store for me?" We are capable of doing bad things, very bad things, but please, do not despair: the Father is always there waiting for us! Come back! Come back! This is the word: Come back! Come back home because the Father is waiting for me. And if I am a great sinner, he will celebrate the more.

—Address, Meeting with Asian Youth, Republic of Korea, August 15, 2014

—For Reflection—

What was your reaction as you read about the Father's cry for us to come back to him when we have strayed? Did his invitation stir up fears in your heart that have prevented you from coming back to him?

Are you afraid of the Father's reaction to those dark and broken places?

What, instead, does this passage say is the truth of his reaction to our sins?

The Mercy of the Confessional

God's mercy is very real and we are all called to experience it firsthand. When I was seventeen years old, it happened one day that, as I was about to go out with friends, I decided to stop into a church first. I met a priest there who inspired great confidence, and I felt the desire to open my heart in Confession. That meeting changed my life! I discovered that when we open our hearts with humility and transparency, we can contemplate God's mercy in a very concrete way. I felt certain that, in the person of that priest, God was already waiting for me even before I took the step of entering that church. . . .

It is so wonderful to feel the merciful embrace of the Father in the Sacrament of Reconciliation, to discover that the confessional is a place of mercy, and to allow ourselves to be touched by the merciful love of the Lord who always forgives us!

You, dear young man, dear young woman, have you ever felt the gaze of everlasting love upon you, a gaze that looks beyond your sins, limitations, and failings, and continues to have faith in you and to look upon your life with hope? Do you realize how precious you are to God, who has given you everything out of love? St. Paul tells us that "God proves his love for us in that, while we were still sinners, Christ died for us" (Romans 5:8). Do we really understand the power of these words?. . .

It is in the Lord, who gave his life for us on the cross, that we will always find that unconditional love which sees our lives as something good and always gives us the chance to start again.

—Message for the Thirty-First World Youth Day, August 15, 2015

—For Reflection—

What is your attitude toward Confession?

What wounds or fears in your heart keep you from fully embracing the mercy of God inConfession?

What is one step you can take to heal your understanding of Confession?

Never Give Up

All of us have made mistakes and been caught up in misunderstandings, a thousand of them. Happy, then, are those who can help others when they make mistakes, when they experience misunderstandings. They are true friends, they do not give up on anyone. They are the pure of heart, the ones who can look beyond the little things and overcome difficulties. Happy above all are the ones who can see the good in other people.

—Address, Meeting with Young People, Asunción, Paraguay, July 12, 2015

—For Reflection—

Have there been people in your life who helped you overcome your mistakes, people who didn't give up on you? Which of their actions or words meant the most to you?

Have you made mistakes that are preventing you from helping others overcome their mistakes, perhaps because you are ashamed or don't want to admit your failures?

In what specific ways might the Lord be inviting you to become more merciful and self-giving to your friends?

The Grace to Forgive

Is it possible to forgive totally? It is a grace we must ask of the Lord. We, by ourselves, cannot: we make the effort, . . . but forgiveness is a grace that the Lord gives you. Forgiving your enemy, forgiving those who have hurt you and those who have done you harm.

When Jesus in the Gospel tells us, "If anyone slaps you on the right cheek, turn to him the other also," it means this: leave this wisdom of forgiveness, which is a grace, in the hands of the Lord. But we must also do our part to forgive.

—Dialogue with Italian Young People, World Youth Day,
Kraków, Poland, July 27, 2016

—For Reflection—

Are you trying to forgive someone by your own strength and not making much progress? Pause now, and invite the Lord to give you the necessary grace so that you can forgive.

Do you believe that total forgiveness is possible?

What does God's desire for total forgiveness say about him and about the life he invites you to live here and now?

Bands of Love

The biblical concept of mercy . . . includes the tangible presence of love that is faithful, freely given, and able to forgive. In the following passage from Hosea, we have a beautiful example of God's love, which the prophet compares to that of a father for his child:

> When Israel was a child I loved him; out of Egypt I called my son. The more I called them, the farther they went from me. . . . Yet it was I who taught Ephraim to walk, who took them in my arms; I drew them with human cords, with bands of love; I fostered them like one who raises an infant to his cheeks. . . . I stooped to feed my child. (Hosea 11:1-4)

Despite the child's wrong attitude that deserves punishment, a father's love is faithful. He always forgives his repentant children. We see here how forgiveness is always included in mercy. . . .

Our Lord's mercy can be seen especially when he bends down to human misery and shows his compassion for those in need of understanding, healing, and forgiveness. Everything in Jesus speaks of mercy. Indeed, he himself *is* mercy.

—Message for the Thirty-First World Youth Day, August 15, 2015

—For Reflection—

Have you experienced God's fatherly love for you as his child? If not, have you prayed for the grace to know him as your loving Father? How can you grow in your identity as his child?

If you see God as a god of punishment, and fear is holding you back, what might God want to say to you about that?

Do you have father figures in your life who are models of our merciful, compassionate Father? How have they reflected God's love to you?

The Other Person's Shoes

As the saying goes: "When you get angry, you lose." Don't let your heart give in to anger and resentment. Happy are the merciful. Happy are those who know how to put themselves in someone else's shoes, those who are able to embrace, to forgive. We have all experienced this at one time or another. And how beautiful it is! It is like getting our lives back, getting a new chance.

Nothing is more beautiful than to have a new chance. It is as if life can start all over again.

—Address, Meeting with Young People, Asunción, Paraguay, July 12, 2015

—For Reflection—

What areas of anger, resentment, or bitterness are currently weighing you down? How is the Lord inviting you to surrender these?

Why is it tempting to hold on to anger and bitterness?

What kind of "new chance" might the Lord be wanting to give you right now?

Chapter 4

•

FAITH, HOPE, AND LOVE

A Full-Flavored Life

"Put on faith": what does this mean? When we prepare a plate of food and we see that it needs salt, well, we "put on" salt; when it needs oil, then you "put on" oil. "To put on," that is, to place on top of, to pour over.

And so it is in our life, dear young friends: if we want it to have real meaning and fulfillment, as you want and as you deserve, I say to each one of you, "Put on faith," and life will take on a new flavor, life will have a compass to show you the way; "put on hope," and every one of your days will be enlightened and your horizon will no longer be dark, but luminous; "put on love," and your life will be like a house built on rock; your journey will be joyful because you will find many friends to journey with you. Put on faith, put on hope, put on love! . . .

But who can give us all this? In the Gospel we hear the answer: Christ. "This is my Son, my chosen one. Listen to him!" Jesus brings God to us and us to God. With him our life is transformed and renewed, and we can see reality with new eyes, from Jesus' standpoint, with his own eyes (cf. *Lumen Fidei*, 18).

For this reason, I say to every one of you today: "Put on Christ!" in your life, and you will find a friend in whom you can always trust; "put on Christ," and you will see the wings of hope spreading and letting you journey with joy towards the future; "put on Christ," and your life will be full of his love; it will be a fruitful life.

—Homily, World Youth Day, Rio de Janeiro, Brazil, July 25, 2013

—For Reflection—

Is there something different about those around you—priests, religious brothers and sisters, lay people—who follow Christ with everything they have?

Do you want what they have—that peace and that joy? This week, look for one opportunity each day to put on faith, hope, and love and then evaluate the effects of your choices on those around you and on your fruitfulness for Christ.

Radical and Revolutionary

Faith accomplishes a revolution in us, one which we can call Copernican; it removes us from the center and puts God at the center; faith immerses us in his love and gives us security, strength, and hope. Seemingly, nothing has changed; yet, in the depths of our being, everything is different.

With God, peace, consolation, gentleness, courage, serenity and joy, which are all fruits of the Holy Spirit (cf. Galatians 5:22), find a home in our heart; then our very being is transformed; our way of thinking and acting is made new; it becomes Jesus' own, God's own, way of thinking and acting.

Dear friends, faith is revolutionary and today I ask you: are you open to entering into this revolutionary wave of faith? Only by entering into this wave will your young lives make sense and so be fruitful!

—Homily, World Youth Day, Rio de Janeiro, Brazil, July 25, 2013

—For Reflection—

Do you wonder about who God made you to be? Jesus tells us, "I came that they may have life, and have it abundantly" (John 10:10, RSV). Do you dream about this abundant life with Christ and what it might look like for you?

Take the time now to consider if your experience of faith has radically changed you and if it continues to change you, day by day.

What can you do to have an even more revolutionary faith?

Undiluted

Faith in Jesus Christ is not a joke, it is something very serious. It is a scandal that God came to be one of us. It is a scandal that he died on a cross. It is a scandal: the scandal of the cross. The cross continues to provoke scandal. But it is the one sure path, the path of the cross, the path of Jesus, the path of the Incarnation of Jesus.

Please do not water down your faith in Jesus Christ. We dilute fruit drinks—orange, apple, or banana juice—but please do not drink a diluted form of faith. Faith is whole and entire, not something that you water down. It is faith in Jesus. It is faith in the Son of God made man, who loved me and who died for me. . . . Do not "water down" your faith in Jesus Christ.

—Meeting with Young People from Argentina, World Youth Day, Rio de Janeiro, Brazil, July 25, 2013

—For Reflection—

Do you leave your faith at church, at Mass, or in your youth group? Or, recognizing the power of undiluted faith, do you bring Jesus home with you—to your family members, your classmates, and your friends who have not yet experienced the love of God as you have? If your faith is "whole and entire," you will find yourself able to lead others on the one sure path through this life—the path of Jesus.

Christian Hope

Christian hope is not simply optimism; it is much more. It is rooted in the new life we have received in Jesus Christ. St. Paul tells us that hope will not disappoint us, because God's love was poured into our hearts by the Holy Spirit at our baptism (cf. Romans 5:5).

This hope enables us to trust in Christ's promises, to trust in the power of his love, his forgiveness, his friendship. That love opens the door to new life. Whenever you experience a problem, a setback, a failure, you must anchor your heart in that love, for it has the power to turn death into life and to banish every evil.

—Address, Meeting with Young People,
Kampala, Uganda, November 28, 2015

—For Reflection—

The virtue of hope can keep you from getting discouraged when things are tough. Do you have friends who encourage you to live in hope and to follow Christ more closely, or do your friends drag you down and away from the promises of God?

What can you do—think about your speech or your actions—to become the kind of friend who helps others to trust in God and to live in the hope of Christ?

The Challenge of Hope

"How can we realize that God is our Father? How can we see God's hand in the tragedies of life? How can we find God's peace?" This question is asked by men and women the world over in one way or another. And they don't come up with an answer. There are some questions to which, no matter how hard we try, we never seem to find an answer. "How can I see the hand of God in one of life's tragedies?"

There is only one answer: no, there is no answer. There is only a way: *to look to the Son of God.* God delivered his Son to save us all. God let himself get hurt. God let himself be destroyed on the cross.

So when the moment comes when you don't understand, when you're in despair and the world is tumbling down all around you, *look to the cross!* There we see the failure of God; there we see the destruction of God. But there we also see a challenge to our faith: the challenge of hope. Because that story didn't end in failure. There was the resurrection, which made all things new.

—Meeting with Young People, Nairobi, Kenya, November 27, 2015

—For Reflection—

Imagine how Jesus felt as he faced the cross. This seemed to be a time of destruction, but even more, it was a time of hope because Jesus trusted in the promises of God. When you are troubled or in despair, how can you find consolation in the example of Jesus?

What does the hope of the resurrection mean to you when you are struggling and suffering?

The High Road of Hope

Hope is the virtue which goes places. It isn't simply a path we take for the pleasure of it, but it has an end, a goal which is practical and lights up our way. . . .

Hope is a path taken with others. An African proverb says: "If you want to go fast, go alone; if you want to go far, go with others." Isolation and aloofness never generate hope; but closeness to others and encounter do. Left to ourselves, we will go nowhere. . . .

Hope is a path of solidarity. . . . Beyond all other considerations or interests, there has to be concern for that person who may be my friend, my companion, but also someone who may think differently than I do, someone with his own ideas yet just as human . . . as I am.

—Address to Students, Havana, Cuba, September 20, 2015

—For Reflection—

You might not think of hope as a "communal" virtue, but Pope Francis tells us that it involves going forward with others in solidarity. On a very practical level, then, is Jesus asking you to extend friendship and love to anyone in particular?

Do you know anyone who is lonely and needs someone to talk to? How can you reach out and help generate hope in other people?

Love Is the Remedy

Everywhere there are young people who were abandoned, either at birth or later on, by their family, their parents, and so they have never known the love of a family. That is why families are so important. Protect the family! Defend it always. All around us, there are not only abandoned children, but also abandoned elderly persons, who have no one to visit them, to show them affection. . . .

How do you overcome this negative experience of being abandoned, of not being loved? There is only one remedy: to give what you have not received. If you have not received understanding, then show understanding to others. If you have not received love, then show love to others. If you have known loneliness, then try to be close to others who are lonely. Flesh is cured with flesh! And God took flesh in order to heal us. So let us do the same with others.

—Meeting with Young People, Nairobi, Kenya, November 27, 2015

—For Reflection—

Think about times when you felt abandoned or unloved or lonely. What could others have done to help you?

Today, make it a point to get in touch with friends or family members who are feeling sad or defeated or who are suffering in some way. Bring them the understanding and closeness that can help them heal.

Pitching In or Turning Away?

The cross of Christ invites us also to allow ourselves to be smitten by his love, teaching us always to look upon others with mercy and tenderness, especially those who suffer, who are in need of help, who need a word or a concrete action; the cross invites us to step outside ourselves to meet them and to extend a hand to them. How many times have we seen them in the Way of the Cross, how many times have they accompanied Jesus on the way to Calvary: Pilate, Simon of Cyrene, Mary, the women. . . .

Today I ask you: which of them do you want to be? Do you want to be like Pilate, who did not have the courage to go against the tide to save Jesus' life, and instead washed his hands? Tell me: are you one of those who wash their hands, who feign ignorance and look the other way? Or are you like Simon of Cyrene, who helped Jesus to carry that heavy wood, or like Mary and the other women, who were not afraid to accompany Jesus all the way to the end, with love and tenderness? . . .

Jesus is looking at you now and is asking you: do you want to help me carry the cross? Brothers and sisters, with all the strength of your youth, how will you respond to him?

—Way of the Cross with Young People, World Youth Day,
Rio de Janeiro, Brazil, July 26, 2013

—For Reflection—

Do you want to be one of those who looks away from the sufferings of others, or one of those who lends a hand? How is that inclination to give or withhold mercy apparent in your day-to-day life?

Are you actively causing anyone pain by using them for personal gain and for pleasure?

What can you do to change this dynamic so that you are helping them, willing their good, and caring for them?

Be a Rebel

Youth is a time of life when your desire for a love which is genuine, beautiful and expansive begins to blossom in your hearts. How powerful is this ability to love and to be loved! Do not let this precious treasure be debased, destroyed or spoiled. That is what happens when we start to use our neighbors for our own selfish ends, even as objects of pleasure. Hearts are broken and sadness follows upon these negative experiences.

I urge you: Do not be afraid of true love, the love that Jesus teaches us and which St. Paul describes as "patient and kind." Paul says:

Love is not jealous or boastful; it is not arrogant or rude. Love does not insist on its own way; it is not irritable or resentful; it does not rejoice at wrong, but rejoices in the right. Love bears all things, believes all things, hopes all things, endures all things. (1 Corinthians 13:4-8)

In encouraging you to rediscover the beauty of the human vocation to love, I also urge you to rebel against the widespread tendency to reduce love to something banal, reducing it to its sexual aspect alone, deprived of its essential characteristics of beauty, communion, fidelity and responsibility.

Dear young friends, "in a culture of relativism and the ephemeral, many preach the importance of 'enjoying' the moment. They say that it is not worth making a life-long commitment, making a definitive decision, 'for ever,' because we do not know what tomorrow will bring. I ask you, instead . . . to rebel against this culture that sees everything as temporary and that ultimately believes you are incapable of responsibility, that believes you are incapable of true love. I have confidence in you and I pray for you" (Meeting with the Volunteers of the Twenty-Eighth World Youth Day, July 28, 2013). . . .

If you allow yourselves to discover the rich teachings of the Church on love, you will discover that Christianity does not consist of a series of prohibitions which stifle our desire for happiness, but rather a project for life capable of captivating our hearts.

—Message for the Thirtieth World Youth Day, January 31, 2015

—For Reflection—

Do not be afraid of true love—love that bears, hopes, and endures all things. This is your vocation. If you are tempted to reduce love to something less than this, make a commitment to discover some of the Church's teachings on love. These teachings, joined with prayer and Confession, can help you effectively rebel against what passes for love in today's culture.

Chapter 5

•

FINDING YOUR PATH: VOCATIONS AND THE CALL OF GOD

Speak, Lord

Dear young people, some of you may not yet know what you will do with your lives. Ask the Lord, and he will show you the way. The young Samuel kept hearing the voice of the Lord who was calling him, but he did not understand or know what to say, yet with the help of the priest Eli, in the end he answered, "Speak, Lord, for I am listening" (cf. 1 Samuel 3:1-10). You, too, can ask the Lord, "What do you want me to do? What path am I to follow?"

—Meeting with World Youth Day Volunteers,
Rio de Janeiro, Brazil, July 28, 2013

—For Reflection—

In what ways have you heard the voice of the Lord calling you? How did you answer?

If you have answered, "Speak, Lord, for I am listening," how did your prayer progress?

What fears did you have in that process? What joys?

The High Calling of Marriage

When a man and woman celebrate the Sacrament of Matrimony, God as it were "is mirrored" in them; he impresses in them his own features and the indelible character of his love. Marriage is the icon of God's love for us. Indeed, God is communion too: the three Persons of the Father, the Son, and the Holy Spirit live eternally in perfect unity. And this is precisely the mystery of Matrimony: God makes of the two spouses one single life.

—Audience, Catechesis on Marriage, April 2, 2014

—For Reflection—

Do you know any married couples whose love is an example of God's own communion of unifying love? What specific aspects of their marriages reveal this love the most?

Why do you think so many marriages today do not mirror God's love as they ought?

What are some small, practical things that you can begin doing today to practice and discern the love it takes to live a life that is unified with God's love?

The Joy of the Priesthood

This is what I would like to say to young priests: you are chosen; you are dear to the Lord! God looks upon you with a father's tenderness and, after having caused your heart to fall in love, he will not allow your steps to falter. You are important in his eyes and he trusts that you will rise to the height of the mission to which he has called you. . . . I am always happy when I meet young priests because I see the youthfulness of the Church in them.

—Address, Congregation for the Clergy, June 1, 2017

—For Reflection—

Have you seen priests, in obedience to the call of Christ, willingly carrying out tasks for which they were not perfectly equipped or prepared?

What do you think gave them the strength to do what God asked of them? Was their love for Jesus evident? What was different about those priests?

If you are a man discerning the priesthood, what joys would you want to find in this vocation? What fears do you have?

Mary, the Model of Every Vocation

The Virgin Mary, model of every vocation, did not fear to utter her "*fiat*" in response to the Lord's call. She is at our side and she guides us. With the generous courage born of faith, Mary sang of the joy of leaving herself behind and entrusting to God the plans she had for her life.

Let us turn to her, so that we may be completely open to what God has planned for each one of us, so that we can grow in the desire to go out with tender concern towards others (cf. Luke 1:39). May the Virgin Mary protect and intercede for us all.

—Message for the Fifty-Second World Day of Prayer for Vocations,
April 26, 2015

—For Reflection—

As the model for every vocation, Mary can help you grow as you move forward on your vocational journey. What characteristics of her response to her vocation can help you to respond to yours?

Pope Francis says that her "generous courage [was] born of faith." It is important to notice that Mary's faith came first, before her courageous "yes." Has there been a time in your life when you had great faith in the Lord? What was different about that time?

Finding Your Particular Path

God calls you to make definitive choices, and he has a plan for each of you: to discover that plan and to respond to your vocation is to move toward personal fulfillment. God calls each of us to be holy, to live his life, but he has a particular path for each one of us. Some are called to holiness through family life in the Sacrament of Marriage. . . .

The Lord calls some to be priests, to give themselves to him more fully, so as to love all people with the heart of the Good Shepherd. Some he calls to the service of others in the religious life: devoting themselves in monasteries to praying for the good of the world, and in various areas of the apostolate, giving of themselves for the sake of all, especially those most in need.

I will never forget that day, September 21—I was seventeen years old—when, after stopping in the Church of San José de Flores to go to Confession, I first heard God calling me. Do not be afraid of what God asks of you! It is worth saying "yes" to God. In him we find joy!

—Meeting with World Youth Day Volunteers,
Rio de Janeiro, Brazil, July 28, 2013

—For Reflection—

When you contemplate your future with the Lord, what brings you peace?

Do you know people living out their particular path with great joy and peace? How do they share that sense of peace with others?

Are there any obstacles in your heart that prevent you from truly believing that it is worth saying "yes" to God?

Walking in Jesus' Footsteps

A few months after Pope Francis was elected, he addressed a group of students at a meeting in Rome. During the question and answer period, one student asked about his decision to become a priest.

How did you get through it, when you decided to become, not pope, but a parish priest, to become a Jesuit? How did you do it? Wasn't it difficult for you to abandon or leave your family and friends?

Pope Francis: You know, it is always difficult. Always. It was hard for me. It is far from easy. There are beautiful moments, and Jesus helps you, he gives you a little joy. All the same there are difficult moments when you feel alone, when you feel dry, without any interior joy. There are clouded moments of interior darkness. There are hardships.

But it is so beautiful to follow Jesus, to walk in the footsteps of Jesus, that you then find balance and move forward. And then come even more wonderful moments. But no one must think that there will not be difficult moments in life.

—Address to the Students of the Jesuit Schools of Italy and Albania, Paul VI Audience Hall, June 7, 2013

—For Reflection—

Every vocation is a specific call to live within the love of the Trinity. What are some of the challenges all vocations might encounter to remaining within that Trinitarian love? If you know of a saint who found it hard to follow the Lord's call, ask that saint to intercede for you as you seek your own vocation.

Recall difficult moments in your own life. What "beautiful moments", as Pope Francis called them, followed the difficult moments, when Jesus helped you and provided joy?

Prayer + Good Advice = Direction

When the Lord calls, he always does so for the good of others, whether it is through the religious life, the consecrated life, or as a layperson, as the father or mother of a family. The goal is the same: to worship God and to do good to others. . . .

I once asked [myself the question]: What path should I choose? But you do not have to choose any path! The Lord must choose it! Jesus has chosen it! You have to listen to him and ask: Lord, what should I do?

This is the prayer that a young person should make: "Lord what do you want from me?" With prayer and the advice of some good friends—laity, priests, religious sisters, bishops, popes (even the Pope can offer some good advice!)—you can find the path that the Lord wants for you.

—Address, Meeting with Asian Youth, Republic of Korea, August 15, 2014

—For Reflection—

Pope Francis says that your vocation is not a choice you have to make but that Jesus has already chosen it for you. What action steps can you take today—even in small matters—that will help you hear Jesus and discern his choice?

The Lord calls you to your vocation not only for your own sake, but also for the good of others. Do you believe that God will bless others as you answer his call? What limits have you placed, perhaps subconsciously, on God's ability to work through you?

Who are those "good friends" you can go to for advice, maybe even regularly, to help you discern the direction in which God wants you to move?

The Exodus from Yourself

Every vocation, even within the variety of paths, always requires an exodus from oneself in order to center one's life on Christ and on his Gospel. Both in married life and in the forms of religious consecration, as well as in priestly life, we must surmount the ways of thinking and acting that do not conform to the will of God.

It is an "exodus that leads us on a journey of adoration of the Lord and of service to him in our brothers and sisters" (Address to the International Union of Superiors General, May 8, 2013).

Therefore, we are all called to adore Christ in our hearts (1 Peter 3:15) in order to allow ourselves to be touched by the impulse of grace contained in the seed of the word, which must grow in us and be transformed into concrete service to our neighbor. We need not be afraid: God follows the work of his hands with passion and skill in every phase of life. He never abandons us! He has the fulfillment of his plan for us at heart, and yet he wishes to achieve it with our consent and cooperation. . . .

Jesus lives and walks along the paths of ordinary life in order to draw near to everyone, beginning with the least, and to heal us of our infirmities and illnesses. I turn now to those who are well-disposed to listen to the voice of Christ that rings out in the Church and to understand what their own vocation is. I invite you to listen to and follow Jesus, and to allow yourselves to be transformed interiorly by his words, which "are spirit and life" (John 6:62). Mary, the Mother of Jesus and ours, also says to us: "Do whatever he tells you" (2:5).

It will help you to participate in a communal journey that is able to release the best energies in you and around you. . . . No vocation is born of itself or lives for itself. A vocation flows from the heart of God and blossoms in the good soil of faithful people, in the experience of fraternal love. Did not Jesus say: "By this all men will know that you are my disciples, if you have love for one another" (John 13:35)?

—Message for the Fifty-First World Day of Prayer
for Vocations, May 11, 2014

—For Reflection—

We are each called on this "exodus that leads us on a journey of adoration of the Lord and of service to him in our brothers and sisters." What doubts or worries about Jesus' specific call for you prevent you from viewing this process of discovery as an ongoing exodus?

All your work of discernment begins and flows from personal prayer. How are you centering your daily schedule around your personal relationship with Jesus?

Imagine yourself attending the wedding feast at Cana, and picture Mary saying to you, "Do whatever he tells you." How can Mary guide you in your discernment? How does she encourage and comfort you? What do you want to ask her?

Chapter 6

•

HEART-TO-HEART WITH YOUNG PEOPLE

The Future Is Rooted in the Past

Being young does not mean being disconnected from the past . . . . Our personal history is part of a long trail, a communal journey that has preceded us over the ages. . . . We belong to a people.

History teaches us that, even when the Church has to sail on stormy seas, the hand of God guides her and helps her to overcome moments of difficulty. The genuine experience of the Church is not like a flash mob, where people agree to meet, do their thing, and then go their separate ways. The Church is heir to a long tradition which, passed down from generation to generation, is further enriched by the experience of each individual. Your personal history has a place within the greater history of the Church.

Being mindful of the past also helps us to be open to the unexpected ways that God acts in us and through us. It also helps us to be open to being chosen as a means by which God brings about his saving plan. As young people, you, too, can do great things and take on fuller responsibilities, if only you recognize God's mercy and power at work in your lives.

I would like to ask you some questions. How do you "save" in your memory the events and experiences of your life? What do you do with the facts and the images present in your memory? Some of you, particularly those hurt by certain situations in life, might want to "reset" your own past, to claim the right to forget it all. But I would like to remind you that there is no saint without a past, or a sinner without a future.

The pearl is born of a wound in the oyster! Jesus, by his love, can heal our hearts and turn our lives into genuine pearls. As St. Paul said, the Lord can show his power through our weakness (cf. 2 Corinthians 12:9).

—Message for the Thirty-Second World Youth Day, February 27, 2017

—For Reflection—

Are there situations in your past that you've been trying to forget? Knowing that the Lord does not permit something from which he cannot bring good, how might Jesus have been present in those moments in a way you might not have noticed?

In what ways might the Lord be calling you to play a part in the future of the Church? How might your story build up her story?

Prayer: Getting in Shape, Staying in Shape

Jesus asks us to follow him for life, he asks us to be his disciples, to "play on his team.". . . Now, what do players do when they are asked to join a team? They have to train, and to train a lot! The same is true of our lives as the Lord's disciples. St. Paul, describing Christians, tells us: "athletes deny themselves all sorts of things; they do this to win a crown of leaves that withers, but we a crown that is imperishable" (1 Corinthians 9:25).

Jesus offers us something bigger than the World Cup! Something bigger than the World Cup! Jesus offers us the possibility of a fruitful life, a life of happiness; he also offers us a future with him, an endless future, in eternal life. That is what Jesus offers us. But he asks us to pay admission, and the cost of admission is that we train ourselves "to get in shape," so that we can face every situation in life undaunted, bearing witness to our faith, by talking with him in prayer. . . .

Do I speak with Jesus, or am I frightened of silence? Do I allow the Holy Spirit to speak in my heart? Do I ask Jesus: what do you want me to do, what do you want from my life? This is training. Ask Jesus, speak to Jesus, and if you make a mistake in your life, if you should fall, if you should do something wrong, don't be afraid. Jesus, look at what I have done, what must I now do? Speak continually with Jesus, in the good times and in the bad, when you do right, and when you do wrong.

Do not fear him! This is prayer. And through this, you train yourselves in dialogue with Jesus, in this path of being missionary disciples. By the sacraments, which make his life grow within us and conform us to Christ. By loving one another, learning to listen, to understand, to forgive, to be accepting, and to help others, . . . with no one excluded or ostracized.

Dear young people, be true "athletes of Christ"!

—Prayer Vigil with Young People, World Youth Day,
Rio de Janeiro, Brazil, July 27, 2013

—For Reflection—

How much time did you spend in silence last week? What about in prayer? What were some of the fruits of those times?

How could more time in silence and prayer benefit your life and your relationship with God?

What do you do when you meet obstacles in prayer (not wanting to pray, "nothing happening" in prayer, and so on)? How might overcoming these obstacles be forming you into a better "athlete" for the kingdom?

The Loving Gaze of the Father

A question I frequently ask myself and many of you—many people—ask: "Why do children suffer?" And there are no answers. This, too, is a mystery. I just look to God and ask: "But why?" And looking at the cross: "Why is your Son there? Why?" It is the mystery of the cross.

I often think of Our Lady, when they handed down to her the dead body of her Son, covered with wounds, spat on, bloodied and soiled. And what did Our Lady do? "Did she carry him away?" No, she embraced him, she caressed him. Our Lady, too, did not understand. Because she, in that moment, remembered what the angel had said to her: "He will be King, he will be great, he will be a prophet . . ." [cf. Luke 1:32]; and inside, surely, with that wounded body lying in her arms, that body that suffered so before dying, inside surely she wanted to say to the angel: "Liar! I was deceived." She, too, had no answers. . . .

Do not be afraid to ask—even to challenge—the Lord. "Why?" Maybe no explanation will follow, but his fatherly gaze will give you the strength to go on. . . . May you always have your heart open to receiving his fatherly gaze. The only answer that he could give you will be: "My Son also suffered." That is the answer. The most important thing is that gaze. And your strength is there: the loving gaze of the Father.

—Meeting with a Group of Gravely Ill Children and Their Families,
Chapel of the Domus Sanctae Marthae, May 29, 2015

—For Reflection—

How readily do you bring your frustrations to the Lord? Do you approach him with honesty and humility, or with fear and mistrust?

How has your experience of suffering helped you to grow in your intimacy with the Lord?

Have there been times in your life when you've allowed suffering to separate you from the Lord?

Grounded?

We all know the parable where Jesus speaks of a sower who went out to sow seeds in the field; some seed fell on the path, some on rocky ground, some among thorns, and could not grow; other seed fell on good soil and brought forth much fruit (cf. Matthew 13:1-9). Jesus himself explains the meaning of the parable: the seed is the word of God sown in our hearts (cf. 13:18-23). . . .

Jesus tells us that the seed which fell on the path or on the rocky ground or among the thorns bore no fruit. I believe that we can ask ourselves honestly: What kind of ground are we? What kind of ground do we want to be? Maybe sometimes we are like the path: we hear the Lord's word but it changes nothing in our lives because we let ourselves be numbed by all the superficial voices competing for our attention. . . .

Or perhaps we are like the rocky ground: we receive Jesus with enthusiasm, but we falter and, faced with difficulties, we don't have the courage to swim against the tide. Everyone of us respond in his or her heart: am I courageous or am I a coward?

Or maybe we are like the thorny ground: negativity, negative feelings choke the Lord's word in us (cf. Matthew 13:18-22). Do I have the habit of playing both sides in my heart: do I make a good impression for God or for the devil? Do I want to receive the seed from Jesus and at the same time water the thorns and the weeds that grow in my heart? . . .

Let us all look into our hearts and each one of us tell Jesus that we want to receive the seed of his word. Say to him: Jesus, look upon the stones, the thorns, and the weeds that I have, but look also upon this small piece of ground that I offer to you so that the seed may enter my heart. In silence, let us allow the seed of Jesus to enter our hearts. Remember this moment. Everyone knows the seed that has been received. Allow it to grow, and God will nurture it.

—Prayer Vigil with Young People,
World Youth Day, Rio de Janeiro, Brazil, July 27, 2013

—For Reflection—

In light of the parable of the sower, consider the "ground" of your heart right now. What stones, weeds, or thorns are present in your life that are keeping you from letting your relationship with Jesus grow?

The Lord offers you "seeds" through your prayer and your reception of the sacraments. Do you allow these seeds to take deep root in your heart, and do you help them to grow?

You Can Do It

[St.] Paul tells Timothy: "Let no one have contempt for your youth, but set an example for those who believe, in speech, conduct, love, faith, and purity" (1 Timothy 4:12). You are called, then, to set a good example, an example of integrity. Naturally, in doing this, you will encounter opposition, negativity, discouragement, and even ridicule.

But you have received a gift which enables you to rise above those difficulties. It is the gift of the Holy Spirit. If you nurture this gift by daily prayer and draw strength from sharing in the Eucharist, you will be able to achieve that moral greatness to which Jesus calls you.

You will also be a compass for those of your friends who are struggling. I think especially of those young people who are tempted to lose hope, to abandon their high ideals, to drop out of school, or to live from day to day on the streets.

So it is essential not to lose your integrity! Not to compromise your ideals! Not to give in to temptations against goodness, holiness, courage and purity! Rise to the challenge!

—Address, Meeting with Young People,
Manila, Philippines, January 18, 2015

—For Reflection—

In what ways have you encountered "opposition, negativity, discouragement, and even ridicule" for living your life for Christ? Jesus received the same, especially as he endured his passion and crucifixion. Do your own sufferings help you grow in your understanding of his sacrifice?

Which of your friends have pointed you to a life of integrity? How did they do this for you in the midst of your struggles?

How can you seek to be that friend to others, especially for those who may have no other strong witness of Christ to guide them?

Con Artist

In the Bible, the devil is called the father of lies. What he promises, or better, what he makes you think is that, if you do certain things, you will be happy. And later, when you think about it, you realize that you weren't happy at all. That you were up against something which, far from giving you happiness, made you feel more empty, even sad.

Friends: the devil is a con artist. He makes promises after promise, but he never delivers. He'll never really do anything he says. He doesn't make good on his promises. He makes you want things which he can't give, whether you get them or not. He makes you put your hopes in things which will never make you happy. That's his game, his strategy. He talks a lot, he offers a lot, but he doesn't deliver.

He is a con artist because everything he promises us is divisive, it is about comparing ourselves to others, about stepping over them in order to get what we want. He is a con artist because he tells us that we have to abandon our friends, and never to stand by anyone. Everything is based on appearances. He makes you think that your worth depends on how much you possess.

—Address, Meeting with Young People, Asunción, Paraguay, July 12, 2015

—For Reflection—

How are you currently experiencing division or isolation? How do these lies of the devil keep you from the goodness and love of Christ?

Where do you find your worth? Do you find yourself chasing after achievement, attention, wealth, relationships, success, social media followers, or other things, to prove your own worthiness?

Jesus Passes By

Jesus always manifests himself . . . in his peace. If you approach Jesus he gives you peace, he gives you joy. When you meet Jesus, in prayer, in a good work, in a work of helping another—there are many ways to find Jesus—you will feel peace and also joy. . . . Jesus manifests himself in this exchange.

But you must seek him both in prayer, and in the Eucharist, in everyday life, in the responsibility of your tasks and even in going to seek the most needy and help them: Jesus is there! He will let you feel him. Sometimes you will feel what is only found in the encounter with Jesus: astonishment. Astonishment at meeting Jesus. Meet Jesus: do not forget this word, please. Meet Jesus!

Let us think of that day (cf. John 1:35-42): it is about ten o'clock in the morning, Jesus is passing by and John and Andrew are with John the Baptist; they are talking there, about many things. John the Baptist says: "It is he, that One, the Lamb of God. It is he." And intrigued, they follow Jesus, seeking him. It is curiosity. Jesus acts as if nothing has happened, and turns to them and says: "What do you seek?" . . . "Where are you staying?" . . . "Come!" (verses 38-39). And they stayed—the Gospel says—with Jesus the whole day.

But what happened later? Andrew went to his brother Simon: he was filled with joy, great joy; he was filled with astonishment at having met Jesus. And he said: "We have found the Messiah"!

(verse 41). And John did the same with James. It's like this. The encounter with Jesus gives you this astonishment. It is his presence. Then it passes, but it leaves you peace and joy. Never forget this: astonishment, peace, joy. Jesus is there.

—Address to the Eucharistic Youth Movement,
Paul VI Audience Hall, August 7, 2015

—For Reflection—

What have been some of your most powerful experiences of Jesus' peace and joy?

When you consider your life right now, how would you respond to Jesus' question: "What do you seek?"

The Gift of Friendship

Friendship is one of the greatest gifts which a person, a young person, can have and can offer. It really is. How hard it is to live without friends! Think about it: isn't that one of the most beautiful things that Jesus tells us? He says: "I have called you friends, for all that I have heard from my Father I have made known to you" (John 15:15).

One of the most precious things about our being Christians is that we are friends, friends of Jesus. When you love someone, you spend time with them, you watch out for them and you help them, you tell them what you are thinking, but also you never abandon them. That's how Jesus is with us; he never abandons us. Friends stand by one another, they help one another, they protect another. The Lord is like that with us. He is patient with us. . . .

The saints are our friends and models. They no longer play on our field, but we continue to look to them in our efforts to play our best game. They show us that Jesus is no con artist; he offers us genuine fulfillment. But above all, he offers us friendship, true friendship, the friendship we all need.

So we need to be friends the way Jesus is. Not to be closed in on ourselves, but to join his team and play his game, to go out and make more and more friends. To bring the excitement of Jesus' friendship to the world, wherever you find yourselves: at work, at school, on WhatsApp, Facebook or Twitter. When you go out dancing, or for a drink of *tereré*, when you meet in the town square or play a little match on the neighborhood field.

That is where Jesus' friends can be found. Not by conning others, but by standing beside them and being patient with them. With the patience which comes from knowing that we are happy, because we have a Father who is in heaven.

—Address, Meeting with Young People, Asunción, Paraguay, July 12, 2015

—For Reflection—

Do you look to any saints in particular as models for how to live a holy life? If so, what do you find inspiring about them? If not, take some time to find a few saints whose stories appeal to you, and then learn more about them.

How has participating in Christ's life strengthened your friendships?

What can you do to invite your friends to know the joy and happiness of Jesus more deeply?

Love Is Sacrifice, Love Is Service

I will answer your question: "Often we feel disappointed in love. What does the greatness of Jesus' love consist in? How can we experience his love?" . . .

Love is in works, in communicating, but love is very respectful of people; it does not use people, that is, *love is chaste*. And to you young people in this world, in this hedonistic world, in this world where only pleasure, having a good time, and living the good life get publicity, I say to you: be chaste, be chaste.

All of us in life have gone through moments in which this virtue has been very difficult, but it is in fact the way of genuine love, of a love that is able to give life, which does not seek to use the other for one's own pleasure. It is a love that considers the life of the other person sacred: "I respect you, I don't want to use you, I don't want to use you." It's not easy. . . . Strive to experience love chastely.

And from this we draw a conclusion: if love is respectful, if love is in deeds, if love is in communicating, *love makes sacrifices for others*. . . . This is—let's go to another key word—this is *service. Love is service*. It is serving others. When after the washing of the feet Jesus explained the gesture to the apostles, he taught that we are made to serve one another, and if I say that I love but I don't serve the other, don't help the other, don't enable him to go forward, don't sacrifice myself for him, this isn't love.

—Meeting with Children and Young People, Turin, Italy, June 21, 2015

—For Reflection—

Are you carrying any disappointment or fear about love in your heart? How does this affect your present relationships? Have you asked Jesus for healing?

How have you experienced the challenge of loving selflessly in a world that prefers to use others or to love selfishly? In what ways does the world challenge the idea that love and service belong together?

Learning to Listen

Today we can communicate everywhere. But dialogue is missing. Think about this. . . . Close your eyes. Imagine this: at the table, mom, dad, me, my brother, my sister, each one of us with his or her mobile phone, talking . . . Everyone is talking but they are talking outside: there is no talking amongst themselves. Everyone is communicating, right? Yes, on the telephone, but they are not having a dialogue. This is the problem. This is the problem. The lack of dialogue. And the lack of listening. . . .

Listening is the first step in dialoguing, and I think this is a problem which we must resolve. One of the worst ailments of our time is the poor level of listening skills. As if our ears were blocked. . . .

We must have a concrete dialogue, and I am saying this to you, young people. How do we begin to dialogue? With the ears. Unblocking the ears. Ears open to hearing what is happening. For example: I am going to visit a sick person and I start talking: "Don't worry, you will get better soon, blablablabla. . . . Bye, God bless you."

How often do we do this? The poor sick person remains there. . . . But he needed to be *listened to*! When you visit a sick person, be quiet. Give them a kiss, caress them, one question: "How are you?" And let them talk. They need to let off steam, they need to complain. They also need to say nothing but to feel that they are being seen and heard. . . .

Learn to ask questions: "Oh how are you?"—"Well . . . " "What did you do yesterday?"

You ask a question and let the other person speak. This is how dialogue begins. But let the other person always speak first, and you, listen closely. This is called "the apostolate of listening." Do you understand? This is how dialogue works.

—Meeting with Children, Santa Maddalena di Canossa Parish,
Rome, Italy, March 12, 2017

—For Reflection—

Do you agree that "one of the worst ailments of our time is the poor level of listening skills"? Why or why not?

How are your listening skills—and what can you do to improve them?

How often do you have conversations that uplift, inspire, and console you? Or is this kind of conversation lacking in your life? How might this kind of conversation draw you to a new level of joy?

Care for Creation

You are called to care for creation not only as responsible citizens, but also as followers of Christ! Respect for the environment means more than simply using cleaner products or recycling what we use. These are important aspects, but not enough. We need to see, with the eyes of faith, the beauty of God's saving plan, the link between the natural environment and the dignity of the human person.

Men and women are made in the image and likeness of God, and given dominion over creation (cf. Genesis 1:26-28). As stewards of God's creation, we are called to make the earth a beautiful garden for the human family. When we destroy our forests, ravage our soil, and pollute our seas, we betray that noble calling. . . .

Dear young people, the just use and stewardship of the earth's resources is an urgent task, and you have an important contribution to make.

—Address, Meeting with Young People,
Manila, Philippines, January 18, 2015

—For Reflection—

When did you last spend a significant amount of time appreciating the outdoors as God's creation?

What does the beauty of creation tell us about God, who he is, and how he loves us?

How can caring for and cultivating God's creation connect us to him?

Chapter 7

•

CALLED TO MISSION

Not an Add-On

Those who are drawn by God's voice and determined to follow Jesus soon discover within themselves an irrepressible desire to bring the Good News to their brothers and sisters through proclamation and the service of charity. All Christians are called to be missionaries of the Gospel! . . .

Commitment to mission is not something added on to the Christian life as a kind of decoration, but is instead an essential element of faith itself. A relationship with the Lord entails being sent out into the world as prophets of his word and witnesses of his love. . . .

To be a missionary disciple means to share actively in the mission of Christ. Jesus himself described that mission in the synagogue of Nazareth in these words:

> The Spirit of the Lord is upon me, because he has *anointed* me to bring good news to the poor. He has sent me to proclaim release to the captives and recovery of sight to the blind, to let the oppressed go free, and to proclaim the year of the Lord's favor. (Luke 4:18-19)

This is also our mission: to be *anointed* by the Spirit, and to *go out to our brothers and sisters* in order to proclaim the word and to be for them a means of salvation.

—Message for the Fifty-Fourth World Day of Prayer for Vocations,
November 27, 2016

—For Reflection—

In what ways is the Lord inviting you to be a missionary disciple?

When did you first realize that commitment to mission is essential to the Christian life?

What difference has that made to how you live your life? Does it influence your everyday efforts to bea witness of God's love?

Outward to the Edge

Jesus did not say: "Go, if you would like to, if you have the time," but he said: "Go and make disciples of all nations."

Sharing the experience of faith, bearing witness to the faith, proclaiming the Gospel: this is a command that the Lord entrusts to the whole Church, and that includes you; but it is a command that is born not from a desire for domination, from the desire for power, but from the force of love, from the fact that Jesus first came into our midst and did not give us just a part of himself, but he gave us the whole of himself, he gave his life in order to save us and to show us the love and mercy of God.

Jesus does not treat us as slaves, but as people who are free, as friends, as brothers and sisters; and he not only sends us, he accompanies us, he is always beside us in our mission of love.

Where does Jesus send us? There are no borders, no limits: he sends us to everyone. The Gospel is for everyone, not just for some. It is not only for those who seem closer to us, more receptive, more welcoming. It is for everyone.

Do not be afraid to go and to bring Christ into every area of life, to the fringes of society, even to those who seem farthest away, most indifferent. The Lord seeks all; he wants everyone to feel the warmth of his mercy and his love.

—Homily, World Youth Day, Rio de Janeiro, Brazil, July 28, 2013

—For Reflection—

What is your reaction to the command of Jesus to "Go and make disciples of all nations"? Does the word "command" make you uncomfortable?

How are you living out this great commission to make disciples—and to be a disciple yourself?

Is Jesus asking you to reach out to anyone in particular, sharing the Good News of the Gospel with them?

Dreams and Visions

Life holds out a mission to young people today; the Church holds out a mission, and I would like to entrust you with this mission. It is to go back and talk to your grandparents. Today more than ever we need this bridge, this dialogue, between grandparents and grandchildren, between the young and the elderly.

The prophet Joel makes this prophecy: "Your old men shall dream dreams, and your young men shall see visions" (2:28). In other words, the young will make things happen because of their vision. So this is the task I am giving you in the name of the Church. *Talk to older people.* You may say: "But it's boring . . . They are always talking about the same things."

No! Listen to older people, talk to them, ask them questions. Make them dream, and from those dreams take what you need to move forward, so that you can have a vision and make that vision concrete. This is your mission today. This is the mission the Church gives you today.

—Prayer Vigil in Preparation of World Youth Day in Panama,
Basilica of St. Mary Major, April 8, 2017

—For Reflection—

Make a list of questions to ask your grandparents or other older people that will help you to learn from their wisdom and life experience. Ask them questions that will not only inspire them to dig deep into their lives and to dream, but that will also help you to dream as you move forward.

After you speak with them, think and pray about what you learned from their experiences.

Making Good Things Happen

God comes to break down all our fences. He comes to open the doors of our lives, our dreams, our ways of seeing things. God comes to break open everything that keeps you closed in. He is encouraging you to dream. He wants to make you see that, with you, the world can be different. For the fact is, unless you offer the best of yourselves, the world will never be different. This is the challenge. . . .

Life nowadays tells us that it is much easier to concentrate on what divides us, what keeps us apart. People try to make us believe that being closed in on ourselves is the best way to keep safe from harm. Today, we adults need you to teach us, as you are doing today, how to live in diversity, in dialogue, to experience multiculturalism not as a threat but an opportunity. You are an opportunity for the future.

Have the courage to teach us, have the courage to show us that it is easier to build bridges than walls! We need to learn this. Together we ask that you challenge us to take the path of fraternity. May you point the finger at us, if we choose the path of walls, the path of enmity, the path of war. To build bridges. . . .

Do you know the first bridge that has to be built? It is a bridge that we can build here and now—by reaching out and taking each other's hand. . . . It is the first of bridges, it is the human bridge; it is the first, it is the model. There is always a risk . . . of offering your hand and no one taking it. But in life we need to take a risk, for the person who does not take a risk never wins.

—Prayer Vigil with Young People,
World Youth Day, Kraków, Poland, July 30, 2016

—For Reflection—

What divisions do you see in your immediate world—friends, family, school, your town—and in the world at large?

What bridge is the Lord inviting you to build in the midst of those divisions?

Who can you invite to help you build that bridge of unity?

No Fuss

In the Gospel mystery of the Visitation (cf. Luke 1:39-45), we can see an icon of all Christian volunteer work. . . .

First, *listening*. Mary sets out *after hearing the word* of the angel: "Your relative Elizabeth in her old age has also conceived a son . . ." (Luke 1:36). Mary knows how to listen to God. It is not simply about hearing, but about listening attentively and receptively, and being ready to help. Think of how many times we come before the Lord or other people, but fail to really listen.

Mary *also listens to events*, to things that happen in life. She is attentive to practical realities; she does not stop at the surface, but seeks to grasp their meaning. . . . Mary knew that Elizabeth, now elderly, was expecting a child. She saw in this the hand of God, a sign of his mercy. The same thing also happens in our own lives. The Lord stands at the door and knocks in any number of ways; he posts signs along our path and he calls us to read them in the light of the Gospel.

The second attitude we see in Mary is *deciding*. Mary listens and reflects, but she also knows how to take a step forward: she is decisive. This was the case with the fundamental decision of her life: "Here am I, the servant of the Lord; let it be with me according to your word" (Luke 1:38). So too, at the wedding feast of Cana, when Mary sees the problem, she *decides* to speak to Jesus and ask him to do something: "They have no wine" (John 2:3).

In life, it is often hard to make decisions. We tend to postpone them, even allowing others to decide in our place, or else we let ourselves be dragged along by the course of events and to follow the "trend" of the moment. At times, we know well what we have to do, but we lack the courage to do it, since we think it is too difficult to go against the grain. . . . Mary is not afraid to go against the grain. With a steadfast heart she listens and decides, accepting the risks, never on her own, but with God!

Finally, *acting.* Mary set out on her journey and "went with haste . . ." (Luke 1:39). Despite the hardships and the criticisms she may have heard, she didn't hesitate or delay, but "went with haste," because she had the strength of God's word within her. Her way of acting was full of charity, full of love: this is the mark of God. Mary went to Elizabeth not to have other people praise her, but to be helpful, useful, in her service. . . .

Once Mary had finished assisting Elizabeth, she went back home to Nazareth. Quietly and with no fuss, she left in the same way that she came.

—Meeting with World Youth Day Volunteers, Kraków, Poland, July 31, 2016

—For Reflection—

Can you think of a time when you told someone something and they failed to truly listen to you? How did that feel? What effect did that have on your relationship with that person?

How can you grow in your ability to truly listen to and understand the words of the Lord and the people he places in front of you?

Launched on the Adventure

Whoever welcomes Jesus, learns to love as Jesus does. So he asks us if we want a full life. And in his name, I ask you: do you want a full life? Start right this moment by letting yourself be open and attentive! Because happiness is sown and blossoms in mercy. That is his answer, his offer, his challenge, his adventure: mercy. . . .

Let us ask the Lord, each repeating in the silence of his or her heart: "Lord, launch us on the adventure of mercy!"

"Launch us on the adventure of building bridges and tearing down walls, be they barriers or barbed wire."

"Launch us on the adventure of helping the poor, those who feel lonely and abandoned, or no longer find meaning in their lives."

"Launch us on the journey of accompanying those who do not know you, and telling them carefully and respectfully your Name, the reason for our faith. Send us . . . to listen attentively to those we do not understand, those of other cultures and peoples, even those we are afraid of because we consider them a threat. Make us attentive to our elders, to our grandparents, as Mary of Nazareth was to Elizabeth, in order to learn from their wisdom." . . .

"Here we are, Lord! Send us to share your merciful love."

—Welcoming Ceremony, World Youth Day, Kraków, Poland, July 28, 2016

—For Reflection—

We don't usually think of showing mercy as launching us on an adventure. How can Pope Francis' words change the way you think about helping the lonely or about tearing down walls?

How has the Lord shown you his mercy? How can you help others be open toreceiving the mercy the Lord has for them?

What adventure is the Lord is launching you on today?

Where to Start?

Dear young people, please, don't be observers of life, but get involved. Jesus did not remain an observer, but he immersed himself. Don't be observers, but immerse yourself in the reality of life, as Jesus did.

But one question remains: Where do we start? Whom do we ask to begin this work? Some people once asked Mother Teresa of Calcutta what needed to change in the Church, and which wall should they start with? They asked her, where is the starting point? And she replied, you and I are the starting point!

This woman showed determination! She knew where to start. And today I make her words my own and I say to you: shall we begin? Where? With you and me! Each one of you, once again in silence, ask yourself: if I must begin with myself, where exactly do I start? Each one of you, open his or her heart, so that Jesus may tell you where to start.

—Prayer Vigil with Young People,
World Youth Day, Rio de Janeiro, Brazil, July 27, 2013

—For Reflection—

In what ways is the Lord inviting you to change so that you can immerse yourself in the reality of life rather than merely being an observer?

What would it mean, from a practical point of view, for you to get involved, or more involved, in life?

Who could you invite to walk with you on this path as you both allow Jesus to change your hearts?

The Lord Needs You!

I think of the story of St. Francis of Assisi. In front of the crucifix, he heard the voice of Jesus saying to him, "Francis, go, rebuild my house." The young Francis responded readily and generously to the Lord's call to rebuild his house. But which house? Slowly but surely, Francis came to realize that it was not a question of repairing a stone building but about doing his part for the life of the Church. It was a matter of being at the service of the Church, loving her and working to make the countenance of Christ shine ever more brightly in her.

Today too, as always, the Lord needs you, young people, for his Church. My friends, the Lord needs you! Today too he is calling each of you to follow him in his Church and to be missionaries. The Lord is calling you today! Not the masses, but you, and you, and you, each one of you. Listen to what he is saying to you in your heart.

—Prayer Vigil with Young People,
World Youth Day, Rio de Janeiro, Brazil, July 27, 2013

—For Reflection—

What is one specific gift the Lord has given you so that you can help others encounter the love of Jesus?

How is the Lord inviting you to be at the service of the Church and make "Christ shine ever more brightly in her?"

What is one definite step you can take to place yourself at the service of the Church?

Chapter 8

•

LIVING THE BEATITUDES

Giving the Gift of Self

I was hungry and you gave me food,
I was thirsty and you gave me something to drink,
I was a stranger and you welcomed me,
I was naked and you gave me clothing,
I was sick and you took care of me,
I was in prison and you visited me. (Matthew 25:35-36)

Let us first consider the seven corporal works of mercy: feeding the hungry, giving drink to the thirsty, clothing the naked, sheltering the homeless, visiting the sick and those in prison, and burying the dead. Freely we have received, so freely let us give. We are called to serve the crucified Jesus in all those who are marginalized, to touch his sacred flesh in those who are disadvantaged, in those who hunger and thirst, in the naked and imprisoned, the sick and unemployed, in those who are persecuted, refugees, and migrants.

There we find our God; there we touch the Lord. Jesus himself told us this when he explained the criterion on which we will be judged: whenever we do these things to the least of our brothers and sisters, we do them to him (cf. Matthew 25:31-46).

After the corporal works of mercy come the spiritual works: counseling the doubtful, instructing the ignorant, admonishing sinners, consoling the afflicted, pardoning offenses, bearing wrongs patiently, praying for the living and the dead. In welcoming the outcast who suffer physically and in welcoming sinners who suffer spiritually, our credibility as Christians is at stake. . . . Not in ideas, but in our actions.

Humanity today needs men and women, and especially young people like yourselves, who do not wish to live their lives "halfway," young people ready to spend their lives freely in service to those of their brothers and sisters who are poorest and most vulnerable, in imitation of Christ who gave himself completely for our salvation.

—Way of the Cross with Young People,
World Youth Day, Kraków, Poland, July 29, 2016

—For Reflection—

How often do you give of yourself in service to others?

How often do you serve the poor?

Do you look for Jesus in the poor? Do you ask Jesus to show himself to you in the poor?

Who's the Loser?

We face so many challenges in life: poverty, distress, humiliation, the struggle for justice, persecutions, the difficulty of daily conversion, the effort to remain faithful to our call to holiness, and many others. But if we open the door to Jesus and allow him to be part of our lives, if we share our joys and sorrows with him, then we will experience the peace and joy that only God, who is infinite love, can give.

The Beatitudes of Jesus are new and revolutionary. They present a model of happiness contrary to what is usually communicated by the media and by the prevailing wisdom. A worldly way of thinking finds it scandalous that God became one of us and died on a cross!

According to the logic of this world, those whom Jesus proclaimed blessed are regarded as useless, "losers." What is glorified is success at any cost, affluence, the arrogance of power, and self-affirmation at the expense of others.

Jesus challenges us, young friends, to take seriously his approach to life and to decide which path is right for us and leads to true joy. This is the great challenge of faith. Jesus was not afraid to ask his disciples if they truly wanted to follow him or if they preferred to take another path (cf. John 6:67). Simon Peter had the courage to reply: "Lord, to whom shall we go? You have the words of eternal life" (6:68). If you too are able to say "yes" to Jesus, your lives will become both meaningful and fruitful.

—Message for the Twenty-Ninth World Youth Day, January 21, 2014

—For Reflection—

Do you want to live your life "halfway" for Jesus, or do you want to live for Jesus with everything you have?

What is one thing that you can do this week to start living more than halfway for Jesus?

Measuring Up

I would like to give you some suggestions on how we can be instruments of mercy for others.

I think of the example of Blessed Pier Giorgio Frassati. He said, "Jesus pays me a visit every morning in Holy Communion, and I return the visit in the meager way I know how, visiting the poor."

Pier Giorgio was a young man who understood what it means to have a merciful heart that responds to those most in need. He gave them far more than material goods. He gave himself by giving his time, his words, and his capacity to listen.

He served the poor very quietly and unassumingly. He truly did what the Gospel tells us: "When you give alms, do not let your left hand know what your right is doing, so that your almsgiving may be secret" (Matthew 6:3-4).

Imagine that, on the day before his death when he was gravely ill, he was giving directions on how his friends in need should be helped. At his funeral, his family and friends were stunned by the presence of so many poor people unknown to them. They had been befriended and helped by the young Pier Giorgio. . . .

As you can see, mercy does not just imply being a "good person" nor is it mere sentimentality. It is the measure of our authenticity as disciples of Jesus, and of our credibility as Christians in today's world.

—Message for the Thirty-First World Youth Day, August 15, 2015

—For Reflection—

Who do you say that Jesus is? Does your answer to that question change how you live your life?

Why is mercy about more than being a good person?

In what way is mercy a measure of how authentically you are living for Jesus?

Better to Be a Beggar

The first Beatitude . . . says that the *poor in spirit* are blessed for theirs is the kingdom of heaven [Matthew 5:3]. . . . It might seem strange to link poverty and happiness. How can we consider poverty a blessing?

First of all, let us try to understand what it means to be *poor in spirit*. When the Son of God became man, he chose the path of poverty and self-emptying. As St. Paul said in his letter to the Philippians:

> Let the same mind be in you that was in Christ Jesus, who, though he was in the form of God, did not count equality with God a thing to be grasped, but emptied himself, taking the form of a servant, being born in human likeness. (2:5-7)

Jesus is God who strips himself of his glory. Here we see God's choice to be poor: he was rich and yet he became poor in order to enrich us through his poverty (cf. 2 Corinthians 8:9). This is the mystery we contemplate in the crib when we see the Son of God lying in a manger, and later on the cross, where his self-emptying reaches its culmination.

The Greek adjective *ptochós* (poor) does not have a purely material meaning. It means "a beggar," and it should be seen as linked to the Jewish notion of the *anawim*, "God's poor." It suggests lowliness, a sense of one's limitations and existential poverty. The *anawim* trust in the Lord, and they know that they can count on him.

—Message for the Twenty-Ninth World Youth Day, January 21, 2014

—For Reflection—

Do you have a healthy sense of your own limitations?

Do you try to empty yourself of anything that would keep you from serving others wholeheartedly? Ask Jesus to help you learn to trust him more perfectly so that you can give of yourself to others through your time, your words, and your ability to listen.

The Secret of the Beatitudes

You might ask me: What can we do, specifically, to make *poverty in spirit* a way of life, a real part of our own lives? I will reply by saying three things.

First of all, try to be *free with regard to material things.* The Lord calls us to a Gospel lifestyle marked by sobriety, by a refusal to yield to the culture of consumerism. This means being concerned with the essentials and learning to do without all those unneeded extras which hem us in. Let us learn to be detached from possessiveness and from the idolatry of money and lavish spending. Let us put Jesus first. . . .

Second, if we are to live by this Beatitude, all of us need to experience *a conversion in the way we see the poor.* We have to care for them and be sensitive to their spiritual and material needs. To you young people I especially entrust the task of restoring solidarity to the heart of human culture. Faced with old and new forms of poverty—unemployment, migration and addictions of various kinds—we have the duty to be alert and thoughtful, avoiding the temptation to remain indifferent.

We have to remember all those who feel unloved, who have no hope for the future and who have given up on life out of discouragement, disappointment, or fear. We have to learn to be on the side of the poor, and not just indulge in rhetoric about the poor! . . .

However—and this is my third point—the poor are not just people to whom we can give something. They have *much to offer us and to teach us.* How much we have to learn from the wisdom of the poor! Think about it: several hundred years ago a saint, Benedict Joseph Labré, who lived on the streets of Rome from the alms he received, became a spiritual guide to all sorts of people, including nobles and prelates.

In a very real way, the poor are our teachers. They show us that people's value is not measured by their possessions or how much money they have in the bank. A poor person, a person lacking material possessions, always maintains his or her dignity. The poor can teach us much about humility and trust in God.

—Message for the Twenty-Ninth World Youth Day, January 21, 2014

—For Reflection—

Is there anything that Jesus wants to you give up so that you can grow closer to him? Is there anything in your life that you would not be willing to give up for Jesus?

Are you willing to look for Jesus among the poor and unloved, the depressed and the lonely?

What can the poor teach you about humility and trusting God?

On the Path with Jesus

Jesus doesn't lie to us. He shows us a path which is life and truth. He is the great proof of this. His style, his way of living, his friendship, relationship with his Father. And that is what he offers us. He makes us realize that we are sons and daughters. Beloved children.

He does not trick you. Because he knows that happiness, true happiness, the happiness which can fill our hearts, is not found in designer clothing, or expensive brand-name shoes. He knows that real happiness is found in drawing near to others, learning how to weep with those who weep, being close to those who are feeling low or in trouble, giving them a shoulder to cry on, a hug. If we don't know how to weep, we don't know how to laugh either, we don't know how to live.

—Address, Meeting with Young People,
Asunción, Paraguay, July 12, 2015

—For Reflection—

Pope Francis says that Jesus' "style" is friendship—drawing near to others. Consider ways you can imitate Jesus more closely by drawing near to others, even when you'd rather not.

Do you believe that you will find happiness by making yourself available to others?

How can you grow in relationship with our heavenly Father and with those around you?

Prayer to Mary, Mother of the Church and Mother of Our Faith

Mother, help our faith!

Open our ears to hear God's word and to recognize his voice and call.

Awaken in us a desire to follow in his footsteps, to go forth from our own land and to receive his promise.

Help us to be touched by his love, that we may touch him in faith.

Help us to entrust ourselves fully to him and to believe in his love, especially at times of trial, beneath the shadow of the cross, when our faith is called to mature.

Sow in our faith the joy of the Risen One.

Remind us that those who believe are never alone.

Teach us to see all things with the eyes of Jesus, that he may be light for our path.

And may this light of faith always increase in us, until the dawn of that undying day which is Christ himself, your Son, our Lord!

—Lumen Fidei, June 29, 2013

Prayer to Mary, Woman of Listening

Mary, woman of listening, open our ears; grant us to know how to listen to the word of your Son Jesus among the thousands of words of this world; grant that we may listen to the reality in which we live, to every person we encounter, especially those who are poor, in need, in hardship.

Mary, woman of decision, illuminate our mind and our heart, so that we may obey, unhesitating, the word of your Son Jesus; give us the courage to decide, not to let ourselves be dragged along, letting others direct our life.

Mary, woman of action, obtain that our hands and feet move "with haste" toward others, to bring them the charity and love of your Son Jesus, to bring the light of the Gospel to the world, as you did. Amen.

—Prayer to Mary at the Conclusion of the Recital of the Holy Rosary,
May 31, 2013

the WORD among us®
The *Spirit* of Catholic Living

This book was published by The Word Among Us. Since 1981, The Word Among Us has been answering the call of the Second Vatican Council to help Catholic laypeople encounter Christ in the Scriptures.

The name of our company comes from the prologue to the Gospel of John and reflects the vision and purpose of all of our publications: to be an instrument of the Spirit, whose desire is to manifest Jesus' presence in and to the children of God. In this way, we hope to contribute to the Church's ongoing mission of proclaiming the gospel to the world so that all people would know the love and mercy of our Lord and grow more deeply in their faith as missionary disciples.

Our monthly devotional magazine, *The Word Among Us*, features meditations on the daily and Sunday Mass readings, and currently reaches more than one million Catholics in North America and another half million Catholics in one hundred countries around the world. Our book division, The Word Among Us Press, publishes numerous books, Bible studies, and pamphlets that help Catholics grow in their faith.

To learn more about who we are and what we publish, visit us at www.wau.org. There you will find a variety of Catholic resources that will help you grow in your faith.

Embrace His Word, Listen to God . . .

www.wau.org